One Hundred Poems of

TUKARAM

Translated and Introduced by

CHANDRAKANT KALURAM MHATRE

Cover Photograph
Chandrakant Kaluram Mhatre

Cover design
Nancy Jacob
Chandrakant Kaluram Mhatre

Technical Assistance
Mangesh Ghodke

ISBN: 1512071250
ISBN-13: 978-1512071252

To
My Aai & Baba, my true teachers,
who introduced me to,
like many other joys of my life,
Bhakti Literature!

CONTENTS

Appendix

ACKNOWLEDGMENTS

I would like to remain forever indebted

To Chandrakala, Aruna, Nancy, and Grishma for being my first readers/critics and for chipping in with their invaluable inputs

To the late Dr A V Desai, for being my best book-mate and for sharing with me his infinite knowledge of the world of books.

INTRODUCTION

Every land has its fair share of people who are termed as 'saints' or such other equivalents for godly men and women whose lives are made extraordinary by their selfless deeds. India, too, has a rich tradition of such men and women hailing from all parts of the country over millennia. These Indian saints, called sant or sadhu interchangeably, have fraternal bonds with saints all over the world in regards with their efforts to alleviate pain and misery from human life through their tireless work. However, most of the Indian saints happen to be gifted poets too, which results in a unique socio-cultural phenomenon, termed as 'saint-poet'. Tukaram belongs to this age-old tradition of saint-poets of India. In fact, this tradition is said to have reached its zenith in Tukaram!

Tukaram's reputation as one of the greatest poets born in India resides on his four thousand or so extant poems which he composed in Marathi, his mother tongue. Unlike most of the poets of the seventeenth century, Tukaram did not write in highly Sanskitised Marathi, instead he chose the colloquial language spoken by the common-most people of his times. This has given a distinct vigour to his compositions which appeal straight to the heart of his readers. By temperament, Tukaram is as candid and as forthright as imaginable and does not hesitate to write about anything under the sun nor does he consider anything too holy to be left untouched. This makes his poems penetratingly consistent in taking aim at the very core of the questions grappling human existence. Though he wrote almost four hundred years ago, in a very different social milieu than today's globalised and digitized world, somehow he seems to be dealing with and overcoming exactly the same dilemmas faced by the human populace in the twenty first century the world over. This continuum of human condition is what drew me more and more to the poems of Tukaram.

Despite the fact that Tukaram was a widely revered saint, arguably the greatest of his times, his poetry is not conventionally devotional. Of course, the predominant theme in his poems is that of spirituality. Yet, even at a cursory reading, one understands Tukaram's poems to be markedly different from other devotional/spiritual poems. The reason is Tukaram's honesty when it comes to self-expression. He does not only harp upon his 'oneness' with the Lord or the bliss attained thereof or the knowledge obtained thereby, but he goes on to expressing in his poems his entire spiritual and worldly journey with all its dramatic ups and downs - with 'downs' seemingly outnumbering 'ups'. Resultantly, in his poems we do not come across some spiritually enlightened 'being' talking down to us from his high pedestal but someone from amongst us who has started from the bottom and knows exactly how steep the climb is. Therefore, while reading Tukaram, one cannot help but feel that it is not just the poet's journey that is unfolding; it is the journey of each one of us. As if Tukaram holds our hand and takes us on that path leading to the ultimate goal of human life. Thus Tukaram's poetry does not remain the expression of one individual but of the entire humanity existent in all places at all times!

While reading Tukaram, one gets an eerie feeling that Tukaram is a contemporary poet, that the content of his poems is of the present times, that he writes for the current generations. Thus we come across in his poems all that angst that we today experience on seeing innocent people suffering at the hands of the terrorists, when he exclaims:

> "Eyes cannot bear to see
> Such is the devastation
> Pains of others grieve
> My heart"

It hardly matters that Tukaram is writing in this poem about the horrific droughts of his times that wiped out an entire generation; this becomes an expression of my heart writhing in pain seeing the images of the thousands of Nigerians killed in the Boko Haram attack. It hardly matters that Tukaram is talking about a nature-inflicted calamity, while our miseries today are self-inflicted. Tukaram's words catch hold of our aching nerve like no contemporary of ours can.

This becomes possible mainly because of Tukaram's avant garde, unorthodox stance on almost every aspect of human life that he deliberates upon in his poems. For example, take a look at his definition of what qualifies as a sin and its binary counterpart (called as punya in Indian spiritual/religious terminology):

> "Punya is doing good to others
> Sin is tormenting others".

Similarly if you ask him where God is to be found, his answer will shock most of the Orthodox people out of their senses. He says:

"Holy places have boulder, water
God's truly amongst the good".

Of course, this creates a problem of its own: who is to be called the good? Generations of philosophers have spent their lifetimes in determining an answer to this question and yet a satisfactory answer remains as elusive as it was at the inception of ethics. But for Tukaram, you need not break a sweat on this matter for he declares:

"The destitute and the downtrodden
Who considers as his own
He alone is to be recognized as Saint
God is to be experienced only therewith".

For Tukaram, the equation is beyond any arguing:
the Good = the Saint = the Lord!

This according of the status of God to common men and women definitely is too much to bear even in our own times for the most and can be easily regarded as heretic, so one can imagine what a furor Tukaram's words must have caused in the ultra-orthodox seventeenth century Indian society! But if you consider this to be the height of forwardness, take a look at what Tukaram says while comparing the saints with God:

"Keep the Lord aside
Worship the saints ardently".

Tukaram's poems expressing his experiences as a spiritually enlightened being, too, bear his distinct stamp. Inherently difficult to capture in words, these experiences in his poems are generally categorized as mystic experiences and Tukaram is branded as a mystic poet. However, when one reads these poems intensively as well as extensively, one realizes that actually there is not much that can be labeled as mystic in these poems. Tukaram's concept of 'salvation' or 'oneness' with God is that of being one with His creation as he describes in this poem:

"Became part of every being
'Me' and 'mine' cast away".

This is the state of his mind that gets an expression as:

"Tinier than an atom
Tuka is as vast as the sky".

What is significant to note is the fact that Tukaram does not claim to have reached to this ultimate state over night. There are apparently visible stages —which a common man and woman can easily relate with - in this journey that he painstakingly undertook, one of which he has portrayed in these words:

> "Trees, creepers are our
> Kindred, also wild beasts
> And birds singing
> Melodiously".

Before becoming one with the Creation, Tukaram learnt to be in perfect harmony with it. This kind of harmony with the beings around was not part of Tukaram's experience in the initial stages of his journey. He found the company of even his own people to be most loathsome and avoided it at every cost. The extent of his distaste for others has got an outpour in these embittered words:

> "Plague is other people
> Utterly unholy".

It is an exhilarating journey that Tukaram begins from this point as a recluse who keeps other people at quite a foreboding distance. The altitude that he attains rising from this personal abyss makes each of his readers gain hope that not everything is lost for them, that they too can attain redemption and even salvation which Tukaram describes as:

> "With bliss brimmed
> All three worlds
> Oneness with the Creation
> I relished".

However, it is not only their subject matter that makes the poems of Tukaram the epitome of Indian literature that they are. These poems are equally commendable for their form too. In fact, Tukaram is perhaps the most form-conscious poet ever born in India. He has experimented extensively with the form of his poems, perfecting what is traditionally known as abhang. Before Tukaram, abhang were being written in Marathi for at least three centuries by a large number of proficient practitioners of this form and yet Tukaram could not only write significant poems in this form but actually took the form to unforeseen heights which tells a lot about his poetic prowess. In this regard, he achieves somewhat similar feat that Shakespeare had managed in England with sonnets; but for the fact that before Shakespeare, sonnet as a form was not exploited by other poets even for a century. How avant garde Tukaram was in relation with experimenting with the form of his poems can be understood by his introduction in Indian poetry of what is called as 'enjambment' or 'run-on line'. Indian poets preceding Tukaram would employ predominantly, perhaps under the influence of Sanskrit, 'end-stop lines' in which the reading of a poetic line comes to a stop at its end invariably. Tukaram, on the other hand, employs 'run-on lines' in almost all of his poems as in:

> "Tuka says just like the baby
> And mother's web of affection".

While reading these lines (especially in the original) if you take a stop at the end of the first line, you are bound to lose the drift of what Tukaram is trying to convey; rather you will have to run on to the next line to make both the lines mean together in conjunction with each other. This particular trait of Tukaram's poetry makes it considerably impregnable for an uninitiated reader who tries to make sense out of it by taking a stop at the end of every line and in process getting grounded completely. Same applies to the syntax of Tukaram's poems. Herein too, he experiments endlessly by inverting the word order in his poems to such an extent that signification becomes almost impossible until and unless you keep those lines echoing in your mind for really long periods of time. It certainly is a painfully long and at times quite frustrating process; but the moment you get the key to the meaning of those lines, you claim a share of the bliss divine that Tukaram has captured in them. And then you too begin experiencing just like Tukaram:

> "In the lake of bliss
> Ripples of bliss
> Body of bliss
> Is made of bliss".

Tukaram was born in 1608 CE in a small village called Dehu in Maharashtra State of India. His mother's name was Kankaai and Bolhoba was his father's name who was a reputed tradesman and moneylender, owning a considerable tract of agricultural land. To this well-to-do family were born three sons and two daughters. Tukaram's elder brother was named Savji while his younger brother was named Kanhoba. His childhood was pretty comfortable, spent playfully in company of his brothers and friends. He was given conventional education and also was initiated in the worship of Lord Vitthal, his family's principal deity, at an early age, since the family had an ancient temple of Vitthal on their lands. He was married in his early teenage as per the customs to Rukhma who suffered from asthma. Therefore Tukaram was married for the second time to Jija also known as Aawali. Till Tukaram's age of seventeen, everything seems to be perfectly happy in this household, when suddenly it is struck with one tragedy after another. First, Tukaram's parents died, followed by his elder brother's wife. These events prompted Savji to renounce the worldly life and becoming an ascetic, he left home never to return.

This made Tukaram head of a joint family and a thriving business at quite a young age and for four years he seems to have managed it well. But the things took turn for worse around 1629 when entire Maharashtra faced droughts for two consecutive years which resulted in unending sufferings from humans and animals equally. Unable to see this catastrophe indifferently as is done by the most in his situation, Tukaram began helping the needy every which way and soon became bankrupt. This, however, did not deter him from destroying the bonds signed by his debtors. Thus, having given away all his material wealth with open eyes, it soon became difficult for Tukaram to run his own household which would make Jija fume with anger. Tukaram, though, had become by this time completely aware of the short-living nature of human life and material belongings, which made him spend more and more time in the worship of Lord Vitthal. Despite being in really bad financial conditions around this time Tukaram managed to reconstruct the ancient temple of Lord Vitthal and began spending most of his time there, singing the praise of his beloved Lord in his poems.

It was during this period that Tukaram began intensive studies of the writings of all Varkari saints (called as sant in Marathi), all ardent worshippers of Lord Vitthal - right from Sant Dnyandev to Sant Eknath - which further strengthened his devotion towards Lord Vitthal. The most important effect that the Sant literature had on Tukaram was that he could overcome his reclusiveness and began to mingle with people striving towards their upliftment. In those times, in addition with the despotic rulers, the common people were also burdened with excessive casteism, diabolic religious practices, economic exploitation and many such evils. Tukaram's poetry initiated an upheaval in the contemporary society to uproot all these evils and soon he had to face the wrath of the so-called higher castes of his times who ordered him to destroy all the notebooks of his poems by drowning them in the river Indrayani that flows by Dehu. According to the legend, Lord Vitthal protected these notebooks even inside water for thirteen days and restored them intact to Tukaram. Whatever the signification of this legend, it is the historical fact that Tukaram's abhang emerged indestructible despite all the might of his detractors and have prevailed for centuries.

Post this incidence, Tukaram's eminence became widespread and his followers took his words to the far off corners of Maharashtra. The social project of annihilation of caste that the Varkari saints had begun under the leadership of Sant Dnyandev and Sant Namdev in the thirteenth century reached its culmination in the sixteenth century when even the Brahmins became disciples of Tukaram, traditionally considered as a shudra. However, Tukaram does not seem to have liked this new status accorded to him and has expressed in his poem his discomfort at being called a saint and even a god. By the year 1650, Tukaram's popularity had reached his zenith, when according to the legends he bodily ascended to heaven. Alternatively, one can speculate that Tukaram simply followed the footprints of his idol, Dnyandev and brought his life to a completion, seeing that there was nothing more that could be achieved except heightening the glory of his own personal cult. It seems from Tukaram's poems and other contemporary literature that Tukaram left for pilgrimage only to never return again. Whatever the truth behind his disappearance, Tukaram remains to date one of the most influential figures in the social and literary history of India, who has left an indelible mark on the Indian psyche.

Lord Vitthal, whom Tukaram worshipped and dedicated his poems to, is the presiding deity of Pandharpur (also known as Pandhari) situated on the banks of River Bheema (locally known as Chandrabhaga) in Solapur District of Maharashtra. Lord Vitthal is considered to be an incarnation of Lord Krishna/Vishnu and as such his devotees are considered to be vaishnav. The form of Lord Vitthal is distinct from those of other Indian deities in that he stands on a brick with his arms akimbo. He is a perfect symbol of religious harmony as he holds a shivlingam on his crown, signifying the unification of the usually warring sects of vaishnav and shaivites. He wears fish-shaped jewels in his ears and garlands made of leaves of Indian basil around his neck. Such is the unadorned and yet alluring form of Lord Vitthal which Tukaram has extolled in a large number of his abhang. Rukmini or Rakhmaai is Lord Vitthal's wife and the divine Mother for all his devotees, with whom He arrived in Pandharpur, pleased at Pundalik for his great devotion towards his old parents. The tradition believes that when the Lord arrived at Pundalik's doorstep he was pressing his parent's legs and so gave the Lord a brick to stand on till the time he had finished attending to his parents. It was at Pundalik's behest that Lord Vitthal along with his wife settled at Pandharpur to bless their devotees and is believed to have rushed for their help for ages. Over the centuries his devotees have come to be known as Varkaris - for the biannual pilgrimage to Pandharpur they undertake on foot i.e. the vaari - and are spread all over Maharashtra and Karnataka too.

The sect of worshippers of Lord Vitthal, in the larger framework Bhakti movement in India, locally called as Varkari existed in Maharashtra, perhaps, for millennia but got its organized form and philosophical base in the thirteenth century when Sant Dnyandev wrote his seminal Marathi work Dnyaneshwari (1291?), considered to be a commentary on Bhagwad Geeta. This was a revolutionary moment in Indian religious history as for the first time Sanskrit Geeta was being made available to the common people who had no knowledge of Sanskrit whatsoever and who were also considered to be unworthy of receiving this knowledge. Yet one more significant thing that Sant Dnyandev did was to assimilate the worship of Lord Krishna with that of Lord Vitthal. He laid the guiding principles for the Varkaris to follow in his highly influential seminal works Dnyaneshwari, Amrutanubhav and his abhang. Dnyandev and his dear friend Sant Namdev toured not only entire Maharashtra but most of India to spread the doctrines of Varkari sect which strongly opposes any discrimination on the basis of caste or gender and affirms that salvation (moksha) is attainable by each and every human being. As a result, one finds Varkari saints to be hailing from all the castes and classes of society. To name but a few, Sant Chokha Mela was a mahar, considered to be untouchable at that time; Sant Sena Nhavi was a barber; Sant Rohidas was a cobbler; Sant Goroba was a potter; Sant Sawata Maali was a farmer. Among women, there had been Sant Muktabai, Sant Janabai, Sant Kanhopatra and Sant Bahinabai, again to name but a few. Spirituality no more remained a privilege of the chosen few, barring everyone else out from the sanctum sanctorum of religion. Varkari saints also vehemently opposed the highly ritualistic form of religion and instead laid great emphasis on righteousness. Thus they influenced every sphere of the contemporary society and brought about long-lasting changes, uplifting and enabling the most downtrodden in the society. In fact, Varkaris proved to be the much needed ray of hope in the gloomiest phase of the Indian history.

All the Varkari saints composed beautiful evocative lyrics known as abhang, to express their devotion for Lord Vitthal and also to uphold the right path of life. As a poetic form, abhang is quite flexible since it allows considerable freedom to the poet in line length and the length of the poem too. Generally, abhang are of two types: one with four line stanza and the other with two line stanza. In the former the second and third lines rhyme, leading to abbc rhyme scheme. On the other hand, both the lines rhyme in the latter which results in aa bb cc dd rhyme scheme. The lines are typically longer in the two line stanza (six to twelve syllables in each line) as compared with the four line stanza (generally, six syllables in first three lines and four syllables in last line). In both these types of the abhang the final stanza bears the name of its poet, as is demonstrated by each of Tukaram's poems which ends with the stanza bearing his trademark phrase "Tuka says". Tukaram, however, did not keep himself limited to these two forms and experimented with yet another four line stanza form with four syllables in first three lines and three syllables in the fourth. Tukaram has achieved superbly lilting rhythms in this improvised form of abhang that he has used with great aplomb. No wonder that, despite its eight centuries old history and spectacular achievements in it for more than four centuries by scores of poets, the poetic form of abhang is still known after Tukaram, declaring it as "abhang Tukayacha" i.e. "abhang belongs to Tukaram"!

Translating poems of Tukaram meant translating all this culture and tradition that Tukaram bears forth in his poems. Translating a language into another is a challenge in itself. Tukaram's translator has to face one more daunting challenge of translating the culture and tradition that he loads each of his word with. In my efforts, I was standing on the shoulders of two giants in form of J. Nelson Fraser (in collaboration with K B Marathe) and Dilip Chitre who have attempted translations of poems of Tukaram in their landmark works, The Poems of Tukaram (1909-15) and Says Tuka (1991) respectively. Whether I have succeeded in my efforts to carry forward the herculean task begun by these stalwarts is to be decided by my readers. I take solace in the fact that I stand in the shelter of these great minds.

Navi Mumbai
Jan, 2015   Chandrakant Kaluram Mhatre

POEMS OF TUKARAM

1

Sublime is this Form
Standing on the Brick
Resting His hands
On His hips

Basil garlands in neck
Draped in yellow sarong
Ever I adore
This Form alone

Fish-shaped jewels
Sparkle in His ears
Kaustubh*, the divine gem
Adorns His neck

Tuka says for me
This is all the bliss
To behold fondly
His majestic face!

......
* Vitthal whom Tukaram is describing in this poem is considered to
be the incarnation of Lord Vishnu, hence a number of Vishnu's
characteristics and names are attributed to Vitthal. Tukaram hails
Vitthal by a plethora of names including Narayan, Keshav, Hari,
Madhav, Shreerang, Pandharinath, Rishikesh and so on. He, like
other Varkaris, also identifies Vitthal with Ram and Krishna.

2

Holy places have boulder, water
God's truly amongst the good

When in the company of Saints
Better to surrender at their feet

Faith bears fruits in holy places
Here the unrestrained is reined in

Tuka says they absolve sins
Let them rid of anguish

3

Vishnu manifests in the masses
Is the Faith of the Vaishnav
Any discrimination is
Unholy deceit

Pray, listen you all
Devotees of the Lord
Ensure each of your deed
To be truthful

Never nurturing ill will
For any living being
Is the essence of worship
Of Lord of the Creation

Tuka says we all are
But organs of One body
All the joys and sorrows
Are borne by the Being!

4

Words are the jewels
That our homes are filled with
The tools that we strive with
Are but of words.

Words are the source
That sustains our life
Wealth of words we give
To one and all!

Tuka says behold
Word is the Lord
Let us praise Him
Worship with words!

5

Give me meekness, O Lord
An ant feasts on sugar

Airawat, the heavenly elephant
Bears the brunt of sharp hooks

Those filled with pride
Undergo excruciating pain

Tuka says know it well
Be meeker than the meekest!

6

Without looking at anything
I saw everything

Became part of every being
'Me' and 'mine' caste away

Took without taking
Hands and legs having laid to rest

Consumed without eating
Tongue savouring tastes

Without uttering words
Made known that was hidden

Without ears hearing
Tuka says came to mind.

7

The destitute and the downtrodden
Who considers as his own

He alone is to be recognised as Saint
God is to be experienced only therewith

Tender through and through is butter
So is the heart of the good

Those who are forsaken
He takes them in loving embrace

Mercy meant for own son
He shows to servants and maids too

Tuka says can't praise him enough
He is the Lord incarnate

8

What a great love my Vithoba has
The Lord Himself became Guru

He provides for all the bodily desires
In the end carries to His heavenly abode

Standing behind and in front, He protects
By shielding from all calamities

Those whose survival is riddled with hardships
Holding their hands, He guides them

Tuka says those who do not believe this
Should consult with the Puranas

9

Gracious the good
That you are, O Saints
Grant me just this
Grace of yours

Do remember me
To Pandurang
Please convey to Him
My humble request

Endless offender
Sinner of a kind I am
But do not separate me
From Your feet

Tuka says if
You plead for me
Then Hari will not
Forsake me

10

Who sends an invitation
To an ant's house?
Just on seeing jaggery
There it arrives

Is a benefactor hindered
Without a supplicant?
He simply finds one
For his own good

Do food and water
Ask to be eaten up?
It is the hungry
Who goes zestfully

Sufferer of a malady
Runs to the doctor's
For the sake of alleviation
Of his affliction

Tuka says who wish
To make life fruitful
They nurture a love
For the Lord's praise

11

Everywhere I go
You are my companion
Making me walk
My hand held

I walk down the path
Banking on you
All my burdens
Are borne by you

Whatever I blabber
You make it signify
Freed of inhibitions, Lord
You've made me bold

All the common folk
And the administrators
Have become mine
Loving kith and kin

Tuka says now
I play appreciatively
Steeped in Your bliss
Through and through

12

Our harvest reaped
It's plentiful everywhere
We rejoice all the while
In bliss of love

We got relieved
From everything
Now, all anguish is gone
And fatigue too

The Creation has become
One Pandurang for us
Now the world is no more
'Yours' and 'mine'

We have worn
All the ornaments
Also have adorned
Greatly everything

Tuka says we are
The worshippers of the Eternal
We need not desire
Anything else

13

Tinier than an atom
Tuka is as vast as the sky

Consumed Self, excreted cadaver
The entire delusion of the world

Renounced trifurcation of the Creation*
The Lamp illuminated the vessel

Tuka says now I exist
Only for the sake of good-doing

. . .

* The distinction between the Creator, the act of creation and the
creatures. According to the philosophy of the Varkari sect, called as
Chidvilasvad and propounded by Dnyandev, such distinction does
not exist since the whole Creation is nothing but the manifestation of
the Creator Himself.

14

Blessed is this day
Saints have descended upon us

Sins got absolved, anguish calmed
Miseries have simply absconded

Attained contentment
Mind settled at their feet

Tuka says their arrival at our home
Is Diwali and Dussehra too

15

The fool quarrelled with the oil presser
Angry and uptight, eats without oil

Seek yourself what the best is for you
Do not bear any hesitation at all

Disliked by others, one abandoned husband
Tonsured the head, sacrificed love

Angry with the neighbour, one went away
Dogs filled the house behind her

Mad at the fleas, one set home on fire
Failed to understand the losses incurred

Tuka says angry with the lice
One undressed herself, people watching

16

Always restless
Mind without peace

Avoid the sight of such
Corpse he is though alive

Filth of vulgar words
Desecrates his speech

Knows not a word of piety
Tuka says nor beneficence

17

A pure seed bears
Fruits sweet and comely

Ambrosial speech on the lips
Life spent for the sake of others

Immaculate in all aspects
Hearts like the water of Ganga

Tuka says anguish is cured
Respite just on seeing such

18

I know not singing
Nor have sweet voice
I count on you
O Pandurang

I know nothing of ragas
Or intricacies of rhythm
Let my mind, O Lord
Settle at your feet

Tuka says no one
I bother about
O Narayan
Except you

19

Sesame, rice you burnt*
Lust, anger crooks still intact

Pray, why have you striven in vain
In stead of worshipping Pandurang

For the sake of prestige and vanity
Bore great strife with the letters

Meditation, undertook pilgrimage
Heightening the vainglory

You gave away great wealth
But to tend to own pride

Tuka says you've missed the essence
Indulging in sacrilege alone

...

* Here, reference is made to the ritual of yajna in which offerings of
various grains, ghee, and other edible things are made to holy fire.

20

Mind reins in mind
So does intellect every moment

I've become my own guard
Holding myself steadfast

Whatever arises wherever
It's suppressed at its own hands

Decrement or augmentation
Tuka remains witness to both

21

At everyone's feet
My humble appeal
Resting my head
On your feet

O listeners, orators
All you people
On examining well
Take for yourself

Have opened repository
Goods belong to the lord
I am just a porter
Ferrying loads

Tuka says the word
Has reached far off lands
The goods have proved
To be the finest

22

If mind's satisfied
Poison seems gold

Greatly wrongful excess is
Know it well that's all I say

Mind's restlessness
Makes even sandalwood scald body

Tuka says any other remedy
Agony seems comfort

23

Without a devotee, the Lord has
No form, receives no worship

Both are adorned by each other
Gold in company of diamond

Without the Lord, who frees
The devotee from desires?

Tuka says just like the baby
And mother's web of affection

24

Protection of Dharma
Refutation of diabolism

This work alone is ours to do
Propagating the creed of Lord's name

Piercing replies
Arrows in hand we roam

Neither inhibition nor awe
Tuka says whether puny or mighty

25

Trees, creepers are our
Kindred, also wild beasts
And birds singing
Melodiously

This is why I cherish
My stay in solitude
No vice nor virtue
To be contracted

The sky is the canopy
The Earth is the seat
Basks therein my mind
Engrossed in play

Blanket and a bowl
For the bodily chores
Makes aware the wind
Of the passage of time

Scriptures for repast
Of appealing variety
Multiple courses
I savour delightedly

Tuka says I converse
With my own mind
I only debate
With myself

26

Salt dissolved in water
What is left apart?

Such I became one with you
Within You I disappeared

Fire and camphor coupling
Does there remain any soot?

Tuka says converged
Yours, mine into One flame

27

Inside the crematorium
I find comfort of quilts
Such is the wonderment
Of Your grace

Until and unless -
All is vainly futile
Words are hollow
Just blabbering

Trees, shrubs, all beings
Our kindred, stones too
Only upon receiving
Your blessings

Tuka says now
I wish to verify
Taking my life in hand
O Pandurang

28

Let's go to the Lord's place
The Lord will give respite

With the Lord let's share joys and sorrows
The Lord will relieve of the hunger

Let's burden the Lord with our worries
The Lord's an ocean of bliss

Let's stay close to the Lord
Now riveted to His feet

Tuka says we are the babes
Of the Lord dearest

29

Not telling young from old
Wicked, sinner or thief

Gives all the same taste
Quenching thirst, soothes

Not telling day from night
All along for all the beings

Tuka says fetch with
Pitcher, mug or earthen saucer

30

Artifice of some kind
I know not to charm people

I perform Your keertan*
Singing sublime Your praise

I know not medicinal plants
Miracles every now and then

Nor I have flocks of followers
To spread my holiness among people

Not the head of some monastery
Nor wish any land donations

Nor conduct elaborate idolatry
Having set up such shop

Nor have any spirits blessed me
With the ability to divine things

Nor a reciter of scriptures
Acting, preaching otherwise

Nor a debater of arcane theology
Like the pundits deplorable

Nor do I burn frankincense
Praising goddesses euphorically

Nor clatter a rosary
Gathering yokels around

Nor proficient in black arts
Evil doings of witchcraft

Tuka is not like these
Condemned of the purgatory

......
* All Varkari Saints performed keertans as an effective means of
social awakening. A typical Varkari keertan comprises of singing
abhang to the accompaniment of such musical instruments as veena,
pakhavaj and taal. What sets a Varkari keertan apart from such other
performance is the performer's commentary on the abhang being
sung.

31

Daughter leaving for marital home
Looks back again and again

Such is the state of my mind
When will you visit me, O Keshav?

Separated from mother
Baby longingly looks for

Water deprived fish
Such is Tuka's anguish

32

Compassion be called
Protecting beings
Along with eradicating
Evildoers

Sin be called
Not upholding mores
Contrary arrogantly
Acting ever

Tuka says Dharma
In order to protect
The Lord has to strive
Taking birth

33

In principal
Suffers loss
That is false
Trade

By those people
Why not be embarrassed
Who have forsaken
Laziness

Though traders'
Equal wealth
Loss profit
Varyingly

Tuka says
Act for own good
Not helpful
Provincialism

34

An ant and a king
For us equal beings

Gone are longing and expectations
The Grim Reaper's noose

Gold and dust
Equals to our mind

Tuka says arrived
Home Vaikuntha* entire

......
* Vaikuntha is the mythical home of Lord Vishnu. It is here that all
the Vaishnavs who have attained salvation (Moksha) dwell in the
company of the Lord.

35

Grow such riches
Those desired by people

Still remain; having eaten, fed
No stopping upon counting

Deep goes moist seed
Then alone obtain the coveted

Tuka says the rich
'Vitthal' syllables all three

36

No regard for wood though
Trapped is carpenter bee by flower

Love, affection bound
Those do not break free at all

Clings on to the clothes
Father powerless to the babe

Tuka says faith
Makes the Lord incarnate

37

I kept my eyes skinned
Waiting for you day and night

Deeply impatient became mind
Anticipating your return

I bade you farewell
Thence on this path mind lingered

Tuka says days of your stay away
Departure to arrival, I've enumerated

38

We relish in giving
People code of conduct
Making a fool of
Those who err

What can impede
Spreading His word
What with the fury
Of the world

False beliefs* here
Have no place at all
The Lord's names are
Sharp arrows

Tuka says here
The genuine alone sells
No demand at all
For false goods

...

* Here, Tukaram has used the Indian philosophical term avidya
which signifies the concept of Maya or "the Ultimate Illusion" which
for the Varkaris is but the Manifestation of the Supreme Being.
Avidya, here, also signifies all sorts of ritual-ridden and exploitative
religious practices prevalent in Tukaram's times.

39

Being paid to weep over
No tears and yearning

Such devotion be called?
Nothing but a facade

When pressed for, shows faith
To turn back ever ready

Flame of a firefly
Tuka says can't light a lamp

40

The meaning of Vedas
We alone comprehend
Others only carry
Burdens on head

Pleasure of eating
Not just on seeing
Payload, carries valuables
Daily-wager

Crux of creation
Nurturing destruction
Those who seize
The Essence is theirs

Tuka says came
On its own accord
The Fruit in our hands
Root stricken

41

Rock the Lord
Rock the doorstep
Worship for one
Treading the other

The essence is Faith
The essence is Faith
The experienced, the Lord
Themselves became

Waters varied
But no difference
Ganga's sweet, others'
Taste have none?

Tuka says this
The secret of the pious
Splitting theology
For the rest

42

I believe in the Lord
Hence I uphold the faith

Makes my tongue speak
He who holds the Earth

Not gleaned words these
Echoes of my own judgement

Have not strived for
Any glory or vanity

Those fortunate few
Will comprehend the truth

Tuka say the stream
Is genuine of origin

43

Good news from the son
As listens the mother

Such should be state of my mind
Singing, hearing the Lord's praise

Melody charmed stag
Forgets to run from hunter's arrows

Tuka says keeps looking
The turtle babe at the mother*

.....
* Here, Tukaram refers to the legend that a female turtle feeds her
litter merely by casting a glance at them i.e. her sight contains
nourishment for her offspring.

44

Lotus knows not
Of the fragrance
Bee thoroughly
Relishes

Thus You know not
Allure of Your name
We alone that bliss
Of love comprehend

Mother straw, babe
Milk savours
What one possesses is
To self of no use

Tuka says pearl
Borne of shellfish
Never returns
To be relished by it

45

Sword, razor
Of steel, sickle too
But they differ in
Utility, value

Doorstep, idol
Of one rock
But their eminence
Deviating

Tuka says such
Is not the case
All the Saints
Are the same

46

You are my mother
You are my shelter
I wait for You
O Pandurang

You are my only one
Elder and younger
You are my dearest
Of the kin

Tuka says life
You are mine
Without You, deserted
All directions

47

The game* has begun on the river bank
Vaishnavs are dancing, O brother
Anger, pride having trampled down
Each other's feet they touch

Dancing in a state of ecstasy
Sacred songs of the Lord's praise
The Grim Reaper is subdued
Such is their towering might

Sandalwood lotion, basil beads
Garlands flaunting around necks
Taal, mrudung playing, flowers showering
Unmatched blissful celebration this

Soothed by music, experience Samadhi**
Ignorant people, male, female, the laity
Pundit, enlightened, Yogi, Mahanubhav***
All immersed in One experience

Pride of origin, forgot their castes
They surrender on each other's feet
Utterly spotless minds have become
Rocks have given birth to springs

...

* Tukaram is describing here the march of the Varkaris in a dindi, the procession on foot towards Lord Vitthal's temple that is carried out twice a year with the accompaniment of musical instruments and chanting the Lord's and the saints' praise.

Constant acclamations make the sky thunder
Frenzied are these Vaishnav warriors
Tuka says they've eased up the path
For traversing the ocean of life

** The state of being in perfect unison with the Supreme Being
*** A widespread religious sect prevalent in Maharashtra during
Tukaram's times

48

Bashes, some thrashes
Bows some, worships

For me neither this nor that
Detached from the both

Body undergoes its course
Whatever comes, for good

All goes to Narayan
All that is Tuka's

49

For the sake of fragrance
Shouldn't crush the flower
Shouldn't eat the child
One's favourite

Lustre of the pearl
Shouldn't be tasted
Shouldn't break music box
To see the music

For the sake of its fruits
Shouldn't undertake a task
Tuka says this essence
Make known to all

50

Even while eating holds
Nose like shitting

Wisecracks of such
Make a fool of himself

What to uphold or hold off
Knows not discretion

Tuka says he considers
Buttermilk and milk the same

51

Day and night
We are engulfed in war
Externally, internally
With the world and mind

My soul undergoes
A flurry of lethal attacks
Which it keeps repelling
Incessantly

Tuka says by Your
Name's might
All my enemies
Have been defeated

52

For the bedbug
Cot is mountain
Scaling it is
Such a task

One's worldview
Holds up
A measure
To one's mind

Inside berry
Resides worm
Keeps revolving
Around pit

To kill hunger
Gleans for grams
King, he calls
Himself

Frog in puddle
Eats but mud
Knows not of
The oceans

Tuka says
This is it
World appears
As you perceive

53

Imitating the gait
Swans crows cannot be

Sod off, fraudster monks
We live by the Almighty

Nose-ring without nose
Entire marketplace ridicules

This is decreed by Tuka
Here no one is to brag

54

Without comprehension
Why to memorise
Vainly straining
Over repetition

Repeating incessantly
Meaning has none
All the meaning
Instead, internalise

Tuka says only if
Visited by meaning
Until and unless
Don't speak a thing

55

In the past ample
Played games
Now strength
Subsided

Moves not
Walks now
Vessel empty
Hollow

Upon burned
Visible folds
Cloth bears
Not uplift

Tuka says
Inspecting folds
Catch hold
Of ashes

56

With letters
Strove a while
Fruit of which
Is the Lord

Of everything
Seeks bottom
Being remains
Without remaining

Bearing fruits
Bends of weight
True yield
Such is

Tuka says
This be the Lord
Offerings be
Of faith

57

You have no might
Yours is done at our hands

Verify this fact
Nothing remains to be said

Hiding behind us
You conduct intrigues

Tuka says for Your sake
We have to forsake the world

58

Supplicant has
But two hands
Infinite reservoir
Of benefactor

What to do now
Where to store
This is the dilemma
I am facing

One cache is
Brimming with love
Tongue is exhausted
Keeping count

Tuka says now
Wherever I be
Humbled I sit
At His feet

59

Child's well-being
Bears mother's mind

Such is the kind of affection
Without gains, showers with love

In the womb carries burden
Its every whim indulges

Tuka says likewise
You Saints bear my burden

60

If heart is pure
Foes turn friends
Tigers don't attack
Nor snakes

Poison be nectar
Disaster be well-being
Taboos be mores
For such

Sorrows will bear
Fruits of bliss
Will turn cool
Fire flames

Beings will love him
Like dear life
In everyone's heart
One feeling

Tuka says blessed
By Narayan he is
Recognize him
By these signs

61

Now where to
Would mind rush
Your feet
Having seen?

Anguish cured
Fatigue cured
Everything
Is blissful

Tight embrace
Of taste of love
Hugely admires
My mouth

Tuka says
To our liking
Vitthal is treasure
By all measures

62

Legs bound with thread
Carpenter bee tied by kids

Such you will be bound
Then who will rescue you?

Neck tied with rope
Ape is paraded door to door

Tuka says watch
Bound bear is panting

63

Donkey decorated fondly
Does not become horse at all

Its braying does not cease
Nature cannot be helped

Dog seated in palanquin
Keeps barking ceaselessly

Tuka says such is disposition
Hard to get rid of tendencies

64

In one's stomach is born tumour
So be called one's kindred?

In forest dwell medicinal plants
So be called purposeless?

Likewise body's relation
Tuka says with all kindred

65

Cannot give up food
I cannot take up forest

Therefore, O Narayan
I beg for Your grace

Have no right any
To recite scriptures

Tuka says short
Life entirely an enigma

66

Salvation Yours, O Lord
You unattainable it keep

I devotion prefer
None of that desire

Your reputation
Do preserve, O Benefactor

Tuka says meeting
One enough in the end

67

Utter, my tongue
Sweet name of Vitthal

You take, o eyes, pleasure
Behold Vithoba's visage

You listen, o ears
My Vithoba's praise

Mind, do rush thereto
Stay at Vithoba's feet

Tuka says, o my soul
Do not leave Keshav

68

If I were not a sinner
Would You be the Saviour here?

Hence my name comes first
Then Yours, O Saviour gracious

Base metal defines Philosopher's stone
Otherwise it is a stone yet another

Tuka says thanks to the wisher
Reputation of a wishing-well

69

Now nobody else in mind
Uninhabited land I dwell in

I wait for you alone
All desires subsided

Lost all earlier traces
Gave up all that despicable

Tuka says O Gracious
You are my soul's kindred

70

Listen to me, o daughter-in-law
Don't use up milk, curd

Aawa is going to Pandharpur
Only to return from the town-gate

Listen attentively, o daughter
Preserve the broken vessel

Store of firewood I've sealed
Without me do not open

Sealed storage of eatables
Do not open without me

Mortar, pestle, grindstone
My mind lingers around them

If beggar comes to home
Tell I've gone to Pandharpur

Eat moderate meals
Do not spend too much

Daughter-in-law replied: Very well
You proceed for pilgrimage happily

O mother-in-law, act for own good
Break free from all desires earlier

Listening to daughter-in-law's words
Mother-in-law deliberated in mind

This shrew's intentions are ill
She wishes me to be gone

Why to go to pilgrimage now?
What to see on reaching there?

My children, my household
This alone is my Pandharpur

Tuka says such people
Are bound fast by desires

71

If you become God
You'll make others too
Doubt not this
Even a bit

If you become evil
You'll make others too
Doubt not this
Even a bit

Tuka says the image
Seen in the mirror
Reflection of self
Most certainly

72

The Lord's in laypeople
Have heard this dictum
But we the doctrine
Fail to fathom

Birth dotage death
Who bears the lot
Afflictions, diseases
Joys and sorrows

Sins and good deeds
Pure-impure living
Who defined these
For whom

For us death, destruction
Whilst You are indestructible
How to believe this
To be truthful

Tuka says do solve
This conundrum
Show me nothing
But the truth

73

Wherever I go
Chases me
No pause
Remembering

Has stolen
My heart
Sole capital
I had got

By revealing
Charm to eyes
Made infatuated
My mind

For the rest
Mouth is closed
Ears listen
To nothing else

Words of other's
Remember not
Tongue is drawn
Towards one

Tuka says
Blaze of love
Body brims with
Ceaselessly

74

Failure to abide by
You always chastise
Why not confer rights
O Pandurang?

Deceived a many
Granting divine powers
Such a beggar
I am not, O Lord

Why should I be trapped
Here setting entangles
Once again, O Benefactor
For vanity's sake

I have preserved
Your sacred words
Abidingly, holding close
To my heart

Tuka says tally
I've kept meticulously
Knowing beforehand
Your objections

75

For your visit
My soul craves
Night and day
Waits for you

The full moon
Is chakor's* life
Likewise my mind
Waits for you

Invitation for Diwali
Married daughter craves
Watching the road
To Pandhari

A hungry baby
Cries inconsolably
Keeps waiting but
For mother

Tuka says I am
Stricken with hunger
Forthwith Your visage
Show me, O Lord

* Here, Tukaram is referring to the legend of chakor, a bird in the
pheasant family, according to which a chakor is believed to feed only
on moonlight.

76

My feet Your head
Do this, O Lord, promise me

Seems to be converse
If happens, great fortune

Very precious means
How can this have any match?

Do not decline, O Vitthal
Tuka says I have dared

77

Waiting so eagerly for
Your message or invite
Why doesn't any pity
Arise in You?

O Pandurang,
Lord Resident of Pandhari
Stoking my hopes
You've made me restless

In my entire lifetime
What have I achieved?
Every moment this
Strikes my mind

Tuka says the genuine
Haven't received share
Mortification of the world
That's all my gain

78

So much better, O Lord
Underwent bankruptcy
Good this drought
Caused sufferings

Grieving, got absorbed
In Your contemplation
Became vomit for me
These worldly matters

So much better, O Lord
Woman is a nagger
Good this wretchedness
Amidst people

So much better it is
Got humiliated everywhere
Good all the wealth
Is gone, cattle too

So much better I didn't
Nurture inhibitions
Good I surrendered
Myself to You

So much better it is
Building Your temple
Children and woman
I disregarded

Tuka says better
Observed Ekadashi*
Underwent fast
Praising You overnight
......
* Holy day in Indian calendar that occurs twice a month on which
Varkaris observe fast

79

Kindness, forgiveness, peace
There the Lord resides

Reach running to that place
Stay there settled

Wherever there is keertan
Like glutton rush there

Tuka says worship occurs
By name the Lord pleases

80

Mine died
Great many
How's it You're
Hale and hearty?

Vitho, how did
You survive?
Now do reveal
It to me

Right under Your eyes
My father died
Grandfather
Great-grandfather too

We're ruthlessly
Chased by
Stick of
Childhood, youth

You had good
Time earlier
With no one
To argue with You

Tuka says
In Your Being
I have seen
All merging

81

All the time
In my mind
This one craving
Resides

With His form
Etched in eyes
Time and time
Keep remembering

Worldliness
Is cast aside
Incessantly
Engulfed

Tuka says I
Longed for Him
Shreerang took
Over existence

82

Hunger ever hounds
Makes roam lands after lands

To hide from hunger, go wherever
Hunger will follow there

Spiritual, religious strivings
Thanks to hunger become miserable

Hunger knows no dignity
In front of the base, makes dance

What can satisfy hunger?
Tuka says dies pining away

83

Dwelling in puddle
Frog condemns ocean

Neither seen nor known
Wags tongue envyingly

Keeps bragging crow
Claims to be fairer than swan

Ass claims to be
Much better than elephant

Counterfeit coin
Tuka says value has none

84

Now Your intrigue
Came to know, O Lord
Deceptively making
Me to serve

Loading off burden
Onto Your head
I am banking
On these Saints

Making us praise
Blew Your own trumpet
Who will prove it
To be true, O Benefactor?

By caste a trader I am
A tough nut to crack
No trickery, please
In front of me

Tuka says not
Have experienced yet
How should I dance
Beforehand?

85

Should not say this
But such are circumstances
The world is calling
Upon Your name

Pretentious this disguise
Have set up illusion
Beggar You are indeed
Came to know

Shameless we are
That courageously
Have banked on You
All this while

Do not know now
How You will end
All this exertion
Henceforth

Tuka says at all
You speak not, O Lord
Promptly accepting
My services

86

On failing to tally up
Sits burning candle at both ends

Likewise wake up mind
For the sake of your own good

Having hidden moneys
Lingers on mind therein

For the sake of the perishable
Tuka says you are striving

87

Now by no means
I am feeble
Of lowly origins
Miserable

Mother Rakhumai*
Pandurang father
Purest of parentage
On both sides

Pitiable I am not
Feeble and puny
Nor dependent upon
Anyone else

Corrupt we are not
Unfortunate orphans
Mighty of all
Our Saviour is

Worldly matters
Left none for us
In hiding, Death has
Gone terrified

Tuka says became
Assured in mind
Having attained
Troves of bliss

88

We are warriors gallant
Shall assail the Grim Reaper
Having clobbered forces
Vanquished the vices

Roaring thunderously
Have arrived the gallant
Adorned with shankh-chakra*
Basil garlands around neck

Arrows of the Lord's praise
Smeared with sandalwood
Brandishing victory flags
Bearing eagle emblems

Tuka says the Grim Reaper
Conquered; became languid
We are bestowed with
All our dues

...

* These are the weapons wielded by Lord Vishnu. The Varkaris make
drawings of these weapons on their bodies with a kind of coloured
substance called ashtagandh.

89

The expectant is
Slave of the world
Venerated all over
The unassuming is

In our own hands
It is to choose
No use of passing
Blame on others

The knowledgeable has
Decorum to follow
The unknowing ever ready
For the repast

Tuka says fear
If valuables on person
Thief hounds him
Like a tail

90

Saint I am considered
That embarrasses me

You have not blessed me yet
My own mind bears witness

Ensnared by eminence
Saddened is my soul

Tuka says this delusion
Subdue, O Pandharinath

91

To Your form fixed eyes
At Your feet settled mind

Sense of body is lost
Having seen You, O Vitthal

Know not joys or sorrows
Thirst is lost, hunger too

Tuka says no turning back
Once catching Your sight

92

Plague is other people
Utterly unholy
Gave up their company
O Pandurang

Temptations thwarted
Egotism erased
I seek Your patronage
O Pandurang

Household entire
Sacrificed O Narayan
Source of life You are
O Pandurang

Tuka says stayed put
With Pundalik I am
Hurry and embrace me
O Rishikeshi

93

People consider me god
Such a sacrilegious deed

Now do as You deem right
My head in Your hand, and knife

Right I have none
To be worshipped thus

Mind recognises sin
Tuka says, O my Parents

94

Us torments the world
Is the Lord dead, then?

Have become orphans indeed
Neither shelter nor shepherd

We have to be afraid of the world
Why is the Lord not ashamed?

Tuka says this land
Is deserted by the Lord

95

By my own might
I do not speak
My Mate, the Lord
Tongue is his

Nightingale melodious
Croons songs
Master who teaches
Is another

What mortal me
Can write verses?
But the Creator
Made me write

Tuka says His
Who knows ways?
Walks a cripple
Without legs

96

Bliss of the service
Soldier knows
Therefore life
He wagers

Come may volleys
Of bullets or arrows
Showers endless
He faces

Shields the Master
Amidst an ambush
Then wounds thereof
Decorate him

Soldiers relish
Bliss endless
Pure and prolonged
Through and through

Tuka says these
Marks of the doctrine
Knows the wise
Relishes who follows

97

Soldier is who knows
The essence of the service
Tracking footprints
Secret routes

Protecting own
Tricks the enemy
Takes everything
Confiscating

Allows not backfire
Leaves no traces
Such a soldier is
Adored by people

Such people
Who are exploited
By one and all
Soldier turns soldiers

Tuka says such
Soldiers who has
He is the Lord
Of the universe

98

My own death
I saw with eyes
That was an occasion
Matchless

With bliss brimmed
All three worlds
Oneness with the Creation
I relished

Confined I was
Filled with vainglory
Abandoning it brought
This plenitude

Broke the cycle
Of birth and death
Shied away from
Me and mine

Narayan gave
Place for stay
Resting faith
Settled at His feet

Tuka says made
Known to the world
The whole experience
Undergone

99

In the lake of bliss
Ripples of bliss
Body of bliss
Is made of bliss

What to say
Happened extraordinary
Further cannot go
For the liking

Thanks to foetus' liking
Mother's cravings
Affection thereof
Therein reflects

Tuka says likewise
Moulded is the cast
Experience exactly
Came to lips

100

Only this I ask
From You, O Lord
Give if you can
O Pandurang

To these saints
Recommend me
Nothing else
I ask of You

Tuka says now
Be generous
Put me on the feet
Of the saints

APPENDIX

Contemporary Speak

Very little information is available today about Tukaram today that is not in the form of legends. As such, apart from his own poems, it is the poems of his contemporaries which throw insightful light on great many aspects of his life. A few of such representative poems are translated here to highlight how these poems can become an authoritative source about Tukaram's life.

1. Kanhoba

Kanhoba, Tukaram's younger brother, also composed abhang, providing an invaluable contemporary document which allows us an unadulterated glimpse in Tukaram's life. Among Kanhoba's poems, the most significant are his elegies that he composed when Tukaram disappeared in the year1650.

I.

I will tear You
Apart in tiny bits
Such is Your deed
Know well, You fool

Better if make me
Meet my brother
Otherwise destruction
I will begin

Will die or will kill
Is my resolution
Better, O Pandurang
Understand this

Tuka's brother says
No bond left now
Between You and me
I will stop at nothing

II.

Sorrow has split
My heart into two
Throat is choked
With grief

What did I do
O beloved brother
That made you leave
Me in this forest

Kids lament
With pitiful words
Earth seems to fracture
Such is the grief

Did you not have
The strength enough
To take with you
Your own?

You know well
We have no one else
In both the worlds
Without you, o Tuka

Kanha says orphaned
We are without you
Please return to us
O beloved brother

2. Sant Bahinabai

Sant Bahinabai also known as Bahini or Baheni or Bahina ((1628–1700 AD) is the last major woman saint-poet belonging to the Varkari Sect. She had accepted Sant Tukaram as her Guru and is a crucial witness to major happenings in his later life as she recorded these in her abhang during her stay at Dehu.

I.

With the blessings of the saints
The monument came into existence

Dnyandev laid the foundations
Erected the pantheon

Namdev its minion
He constructed the walls

Janardan Eknath
Provided pillar of Bhagvat

Tuka has become the spire
Sing His praise leisurely

Baheni the flag waving
Has chronicled admiringly

II.

Sings praise of the Lord
All the while in the temple
I listen to him
Day and night

Poems of Tukoba consist
Essence of the Vedas
My mind receives
Contentment

Tukoba's form
Earlier I had seen
While in Kolhapur
In my dreams

That same form
When seen in reality
Eyes get brimmed
With joy

Day and night
Get no sleep at all
Tukoba having entered
In my mind

Bahini says steeped
In waves of bliss
The experienced alone
Would understand

3. Rameshwar Bhatt Bahulkar

Rameshwar Bhatt was Tukaram's contemporary and initially a fierce detractor who was pivotal in ordering Tukaram to drown his notebooks of poems in the River Indrayani. However, once convinced of Tukaram's greatness, he accepted Tukaram as his Guru and remained his vociferous advocate throughout his remaining life.

I.

Tukaram! Tukaram!
Reciting Death is frightened

Glorious Tukaram, the Mighty
Who attained the Ultimate Goal

In water, stone-bound notebooks
Made to float like puffed rice

Rameshwar Bhatt says to the learned
Tuka and Vishnu are not different

II.

Hail Tukaram
My Lord my Guru
Divine Bliss incarnate
Let me touch your feet

Lord Ram made rocks
Float in the ocean
Likewise He protected
Tukaram's abhang

To compare with Tuka
The Lord is the only match
Hence Rameshwar rests
Head on his feet

SOURCE TEXT

Shri Tukarambawanchya Abhanganchi Gaatha. Ed. Vishnu
Parshuram Shastri Pandit. Mumbai: Maharashtra Rajya Sahitya Ani
Sanskruti Mandal, 2011. Print.
***

ABOUT THE AUTHOR

Chandrakant Kaluram Mhatre is a bilingual poet & writer of short fiction from Navi Mumbai, Maharashtra State of India, writing in English as well as his mother-tongue Marathi. He is a translator of Marathi literature into English and is also a keen researcher of folk culture, language and literature.

Made in United States
Troutdale, OR
05/14/2024

19855681R10082